FACING RECOVERY

MUNCIE, INDIANA

DR. KATHRYN LUDWIG

THE FACING PROJECT PRESS

THE FACING PROJECT PRESS

An imprint of The Facing Project

Muncie, Indiana 47305

facingproject.com

First published in the United States of America by The Facing Project Press, an imprint of The FacingProject and division of The Facing Project Gives Inc., 2025.

First paperback edition March 2025

Cover design by Shantanu Suman

Library of Congress Control Number: 2025932104

ISBN: 979-8-9902900-1-3 (paperback)

ISBN: 979-8-9902900-2-0 (eBook)

Printed in the United States of America

10 9 8 7 6 5 4 3 2 1

CONTENTS

PREFACE

Dr. Kathryn Ludwig, Editor
Assistant Teaching Professor of English, Ball State University

Each year I take eighteen first-year students from Ball State University to downtown Muncie to learn about writing in the community. Many come to the experience feeling nervous about leaving campus and skeptical that they have anything to offer. At the end of their two semesters in the "Writing for Change" class, students have completed projects that persuade them of their capacity to effect change, as well as their responsibility to do so.

The co-educators in this transformative experience are the members, staff, and guests at Recovery Café Muncie. The Recovery Café enacts a value that I hold very dear, which is the belief that every human being is precious and worthy of love. It's a belief that underpins my work as a teacher, and it's something that I want young adults to see in action. In coming together with the RCM community, we get the opportunity to learn from people who are experts on recovery and to become immersed in a community rooted in love, empathy, and compassion.

"Writing for Change" is part of the Immersive Learning program at Ball State University. Immersive learning breaks down the barrier that often exists between campus and community through learning experiences in which students work with local organizations to complete impactful projects. The short-term benefit to students of partnering with community members is a sense of purpose that strengthens their academic success through increased confidence and a feeling of belonging. I also hope that in the long-term, students see the importance of crossing boundaries, engaging people with different experiences, and contributing to worthy work in their communities.

This Facing Project began during the fall of 2024. Students in the "Writing for Change" course were paired with Recovery Café members who volunteered to share their stories. Students met with their storytelling partner each time we visited the Café and learned to listen well. Students emerged from those conversations with a meaningful understanding of recovery and profound respect for the storytellers. They learned about empathy, both from the experience of listening and also from the example set by members of the Café. Many students described a feeling that the member they interacted with reminded them of a family member or friend in some way. Others made connections between members' experiences or emotions and their own. For us, the opportunity to enter the Café as welcome guests and hear firsthand accounts from people doing the hard work of recovery was a privilege. The purpose of this collection is to share that privilege with readers, in the hopes that they will be transformed as we have been.

This collection presents stories told by people on both sides of the immersive partnership. You will read stories of recovery, along with stories of impact shared by former students. We hope this collection will make its way into the community to affect ideas about recovery. The message available in these stories is that we are all in recovery from something and that engaging with recovery matters.

INTRODUCTION

Lisa Roossien, Executive Director, Recovery Café Muncie

Welcome to a collection of personal recovery stories from Recovery Café Muncie. Here, you will find many different paths up the mountain of recovery. One person might say, "You can quit if you just put your mind to it," while another might say, "I was powerless by myself. I needed help." At Recovery Café Muncie, both perspectives are valid. We believe in multiple pathways to recovery and respect that if something is working for someone, we have no right to tell them they are wrong. Every person is an expert in their own recovery.

At Recovery Café Muncie, every person is treated with respect and dignity, something our members often do not receive in other places. We have found that treating people as good people helps them to act like good people. Treating people as leaders helps them become leaders. And treating people as if their recovery path is "correct" helps them achieve and ultimately maintain recovery.

However, we also recognize the importance of honesty when an approach to recovery isn't working. In such cases, our community serves as a melting pot of recovery approaches and offers a variety of alternative paths and ideas. This allows individuals to explore different methods that might better suit their needs.

As you delve into these stories, remember that Recovery Café

Muncie is a supportive space where people connect and hold each other lovingly accountable to their personal goals. We do not set their goals or dictate their paths. Instead, we provide the resources, accountability, and love necessary for success all while maintaining a safe community where differing opinions are respected. There is no "right path" – we're all here to explore and enjoy the journey together.

We encourage you to read all the stories, even those that challenge your beliefs. Embrace new perspectives and recognize the truth and value in each person's experience. Our hope is that this book will offer hope to those considering recovery, foster empathy in those who are skeptical of the process, and empower allies to continue to stand with us.

Whatever your reason for picking up this book, thank you. We hope you find it enjoyable and insightful and we hope it brings you hope.

RECOVERING BACK TO LIFE

SEAN'S STORY AS TOLD TO
HANSON HEINTZELMAN

I think a lot of the time in recovery we get lost in thinking we're *recovering from*. We are recovering from bad relationships, or recovering from drugs. I want to show people that they can *recover back to*.

My recovery journey is all about rediscovering what I lost. I had a lot of great things in my life. High school was great. Sports were good. I went to regionals in basketball, Hall of Fame in football, raced nationals in motocross, and went to semi state in track. Academics were good. I took AP English, AP Biology, and Academic Honors in Landscape Architecture. I also did competitive motocross racing and had a sponsorship from Suzuki. But I had a devastating crash early on, and that really took a toll on me. At 16, I broke my back in a major crash. I broke my L1 and L3. Suzuki had to terminate the contract because my career was pretty much over. I lost my stable family when that was going on. At 18, my mom divorced my dad and left. I was gradually losing parts of myself.

After high school, I went to college. I applied to the Architecture Program but didn't get in and I didn't know where to go with my life after that. My friends dispersed to college. I stayed here and it was an extremely confusing time for me. It felt like everyone in my life was

1

gone and I had no one left to turn to. I started hanging out with the wrong crowd. Started smoking. Started drinking. It felt like I was losing more and more parts of myself.

At 19, I started dealing with some real spiritual warfare. It just felt like everyone was out to get me. I would even go so far as saying that the devil was out to get me, at times. I'm a Christian. I was saved and baptized in middle school, so when I started to face real spiritual warfare, I didn't know what to do with myself. I went to the doctor and told him, "I don't know what is going on. I'm just paranoid all the time." I ended up getting diagnosed with paranoid schizophrenia, but I couldn't understand where that paranoia came from. So, from about 20 to 30 the spiritual warfare was happening all the time, and I didn't know why. Later on, I got re-diagnosed schizo-affective and PTSD with a substance use disorder (SUD) of alcohol. It turns out, I also have neuropathy from past injuries. While it was good to have an explanation, it was pretty hard news to take in. I felt I had really lost myself.

The doctors were good at giving me all the right resources I needed to succeed and keep going. They were a big part of getting me started in recovery. I would say I'm still in that recovery. I'm gradually finding the parts of me that I had once lost.

Recovery Café has also been a key to my recovery. When I first found the Café, I came in as a regular person. Then, they moved me up the leaderboard and eventually offered me a position here. It was a perfect fit. I am now a Manager and I'm in charge of the MEND (Motivate, Empower, Navigate, Discover) program, which is granted through the Colts. One of the coolest things about my job is that I'm salaried by the Colts to help people. While they're playing on the field, I'm the guy on the streets using the brains to help people, and using my story to help people.

I am also finishing up my associates degree at Indiana Wesleyan in Science and Human Services. I was also able to get five certifications within the past few years. For me, going back to school and being salaried by the Colts, was and is, my recovery back to life. My future goal is to build a program like Big Brothers/Big Sisters for people from the ages of 19 to 24. Basically, the program would provide them someone just to walk alongside them. If people need someone to talk to, that's what we'll be there to do. I want to help people find the selves they have lost . . . or prevent them from losing themselves to begin with. By using my story to help other people recover I, too, am recovering back to life.

Come How You Are

Rosa's Story as Told to Janiya Woolfork

C lothes mean nothing. It's your soul. So, come how you are.

I try to tell people that every day, to help them through their past. But I didn't always believe it for myself. I had to go through life and live through things to learn it. Learning things was always hard for me, not only in reading and writing, but in understanding the important things.

It was rough for me when I was a child. I went through a lot. It was always a sad house, in a way. I had to take care of everyone in my family— my daddy, mother, and grandmother. Maybe because of all that rough stuff with my family, I rejected the faith they tried to teach me. I was taught faith all throughout my upbringing. I went to Sunday school up until I didn't have to.

When I left my faith, I started to live differently. I went a little wild, since I could finally do what I wanted. In my 20's, I started to use crack for fun but it turned into more. I wanted to have fun after being cooped up in my house throughout childhood but I fell into a bad space. I had to learn that being in that bad headspace was messing my life.

After years of living this way, I said, "Oh Lord, I am tired of this." I came to the conclusion, I got to walk out on this man, and walk on. I

4

told my boyfriend that I had had enough. I lost my house, my money. I chose to be homeless rather than be stuck in a relationship like that. I stopped taking drugs, cold turkey, and never looked back. It was not hard to quit when I found God again.

I found my way back in the light, back into Jesus's light. I made that one step and God took me all the way. I had to learn the gift of light that God has given to me. I had to learn what faith meant to me, not what my family thought faith was. So, I started to go back to Church to connect with the community and Jesus more, which was what I needed. I learned that Jesus says, "Come how you are."

The path that Jesus had for me led me to the Recovery Café. At the Café, I help others learn to love themselves by sharing my love. It's the best thing that could have happened to me. Everyone I meet here is different. People here . . . you can feel the love. I love to be around them. I love to hear people's stories. I tell them, your past is your past. In listening to people's stories, I help them talk it out. People say, "Thank you, Miss Rosa," which makes me want to come in every day.

There have been a lot of bad things in my life. But, now, it's just so joyful. I have my own apartment. It's so nice. I tell everyone, if you get to know that man, that God up there, and you believe in Him and have that trust, it's a wonderful feeling. I am so blessed. I get to see God's plan and I get to share with others.

ROSES OVER ROCKS

NATE'S STORY TOLD AS TOLD TO BRIDGETT NESBITT

One thing my son's mom told me that I've held onto is, "A rose given gets you a lot further than a rock thrown." It reminds me that to receive respect I must give respect. It is a reminder to me to stay calm and collected when talking to people. That's hard for me sometimes 'cause dope has made me aggressive. My main motivator to get and stay clean has always been the family I created, especially my son. If it weren't for them, I wouldn't care as much. I gotta do it for them because, in my own childhood, I never had a dad or much of a family at all. It's important to me that my kids do get that. I know I haven't been the perfect dad but I have worked a lot on myself even to be here today so that I can give them my best.

Dope really messed my life up. I lost everything 'cause of it. I had it all—a nice car and a beautiful house, a family. A single decision six years ago made that all vanish. I did not know that when I went to my best friend's house, to be consoled after a bad fight with my ex, that he was gonna have dope there. I had always been the kind of person to say that nothing can make me addicted to it. I could quit anything at any time, until I touched that stuff. After my very first hit of this shit I was hooked. I was strung out for three days after that. It was crazy because I had only used weed before this, and even crazier that this happened after I had gone to prison. My whole life changed that night.

All I cared about was getting another hit. I mean, I even quit my job so I could spend all my time looking for it. It was a disease and for three years that's all I did. I can't believe I let it kick my ass like that.

I had started to believe there was no way in hell I could ever get off of it. It finally got to the point where it was messing with my mind and making me very aggressive. I don't like being like that. I don't like that side of me. I like to be cool, calm, collected, and respect everybody. But if I find someone who's disrespectful, I'm very ready to fight. I shouldn't be like that, though. I'm learning to have a conversation instead of instantly snapping, because what's disrespectful to me might not be disrespectful to you.

It has taken everything in me to get to where I am now. I had to eventually move out of the city to get away from the drugs. I moved from Anderson to Muncie in 2022 and when I first got here, I still smoked meth. That was until June 17th, when I was arrested. My wife called me when I was in jail and said if I continued using, she was done, and I never touched that shit again.

Family has always been what brings me back to myself. Before the drugs, when I was in jail in 2012, I was on the phone with my son one day and he said, "Daddy when are you gonna come home and play with me?" It made me start crying and helped me straighten up. From that day forward I never got another write-up, never received any conduct or anything like that. I was straight to get home. If I could do it for them back then, I can do it for them now. I just need to remember *that* motivation.

Since June 17th, 2022, I've been straightening out my life for them. It has been hard, but it is what they deserve. I started going to the Recovery Café about six months ago and I love it there. It's such an uplifting and motivating place. Seriously, you can't go there in a bad mood and leave still in a bad mood. I was a companion here, but I was just made a Team Leader. Going to the Recovery Café has helped in my own recovery. Being able to hear about other people's lives and learn from others' mistakes steered me in the way I needed to go.

So, yeah, I've been working really hard to get myself back right for my family's sake. I realize that, once I set my mind to it, I know I *can* do it. That's the main thing, is setting my mind to do it. I'm proving to myself that I can actually do this.

Since getting sober, I feel a lot better, I'm more at ease I guess you could say, and I don't feel so uptight and aggressive. Don't get me wrong, getting sober didn't cure it, but it has eased it up because I'm not on drugs anymore. I also realized I was never a bad person, the dope just made me a bad person but that was because of the drug, it wasn't me. I believe everything in life happens for a reason and if you are a good person you will eventually get good things. I am now seeing the good things life has to offer which has proven to me that I really am a good person.

How Working for Change Changed Me

Morgan's Story as Told to Ruth Snyder

W hen I first came to Ball State, I knew I wanted to be involved not only on campus, but in the community. My advisor recommended the immersive first-year composition class with Dr. Ludwig and it turned out to be an amazing experience. A major part of the class was visiting the Recovery Café in downtown Muncie, which made it possible to connect with people beyond campus. Another major part of the class that was great was working with classmates on a project. I was really not expecting to make close friends in my freshman writing class, but because we collaborated all year long and worked toward something we thought was important, we got really close. There were times when the work was frustrating because some people in our class didn't do their part, or because we didn't get support from people we reached out to. I learned how hard it is to make a difference, but I also learned how important it is to try.

The first time we went to the Café was nerve-racking because it was early on in the semester and I didn't really know anyone in the class yet. It turned out to be a real bonding experience, and we got to hear the stories of the members and their challenges. It was humbling. I knew that people in this world face challenges, but I guess I had never

9

realized just how much. I was also nervous because I felt like I was invading their space. But everyone was so welcoming to the class. I will never forget that first day.

At first the idea that we would be helping to support the Café members was overwhelming. I honestly didn't feel very confident that I could do anything to help. We had to propose a project and it seemed like such a big ask. Even after we identified the pantry project to provide food and basic necessities for members, I was scared that we wouldn't be able to make a difference. It weighed on me.

We did a lot of collecting, donating, soliciting, and other outsourcing. My group divided up our tasks and created one portfolio of everything we achieved. My main focus was reaching out to places in the community like grocery stores, banks, and on-campus facilities. I asked them for permission to place a donation box, to make a money donation, or to be a continuous partner and donate food. I made a spreadsheet, emailed and called lots of people, and helped out anywhere else I was needed.

I learned some important professional skills from doing my part. I definitely advanced my organizational skills from keeping track of all the companies we reached out to. Dr. Ludwig taught us how to write formal communications. That was definitely not something I knew before. I thought to myself, "Wow, I have been emailing people wrong this whole time!" These skills have helped me in several classes this semester and even just in figuring out what I want to do moving forward. They've taught me how to make a good impression when reaching out to someone, and they also reinforced the importance of being well-organized. If you're not organized, things are going to go downhill fast.

It was a truly amazing experience, but it was one that caused me much stress trying to handle everything being thrown at me. I had a lot of family issues and personal medical issues going on that made it difficult to actually get to the Café. I was bouncing back and forth to my hometown for doctors' appointments that prevented me from going and seeing the advancements of our hard work. On top of that, I had a grandparent die towards the end of our project. It was almost impossible to be there for my class and work hard on our tasks while also being there for my family.

Despite the stress, I felt good about the work. I knew that I was allowing people access to food that they wouldn't have had otherwise. Everyone there is recovering from something and some face homelessness. Personally, I haven't been exposed to hard challenges or addiction in my life. I know a few people, but never someone who's close to me, and helping people firsthand really expanded my perspective. Most importantly, that class showed me that not everybody has the same story. Obviously, I knew that before, but the experience really reinforced it. Just listening to the Café members and hearing what they went through and how they got through it, really changed my perspective. It helped me realize people are out here who may really need a helping hand!

Being involved with the Café changed the way I interact with people, especially when meeting someone for the first time. I learned firsthand that you never know what someone is going through. When you look at a person, you would never think of what their past is, or what they've experienced. You have to look at people and recognize that you don't know their whole story.

The Café members taught me that you can't ever imagine how the people around you have gotten to where they are. Those people are your community and you can't take them for granted.

OUT OF ISOLATION

MARK'S STORY AS TOLD TO KYNDALL TUCKER

I grew up feeling like an only child even though I had three older siblings. I was born with a disability called Usher syndrome, which often set me apart from other people. On a lot of days, I felt very lonely and didn't know who to turn to. I love talking to people, being around people. I do. So, it's hard to be so isolated. I love the people here at the Café. I love hearing people's stories. The social aspect of meetings helps me out a lot with my depression and staying sober. It helps me to get out of myself. People have asked, do you think that you have a recovery story? Are you in recovery from something? I thought, what from? I'm recovering from alcohol. But I'm also recovering from the isolation I've had all my life with my disability.

Usher syndrome is a rare genetic disease that affects hearing, vision, and sometimes balance. Because of my disability, it's always been hard for me to socialize with others, especially in school. I had to dedicate so much time trying to succeed in my schoolwork, and it affected my social life. In first grade, I was placed in a Special Education program, where I was in a special needs classroom for half the day, because of the challenges I had. The teacher would come over a couple times a week and do one-on-one sessions to help me retain the knowledge. When my vision issues started, that just added to my problems of socialization and feeling different.

I didn't get much help for my disability and loneliness at home. My parents tried their hardest to make sure we were as *normal* as possible, but both of them struggled with alcohol addiction, making my life at home very chaotic. Since my sister and I share the same disability, we had to lean on each other a lot when it came to school stuff. When I came home from school, I didn't have any friends to play outside with. I spent most of my time by myself, mostly in front of a television.

But I really love learning. My mother was a very, very intelligent person. She loved to read, and that's probably one of the few things that she did for me and my siblings. We all love to read. She was a wonderful person, but she struggled with her mental health. We never did figure out exactly what her diagnosis would have been. Probably it would have been manic depression. Now they call it bipolar disorder.

I pursued my education, hoping everything else would fall into place. But, it was when I was in college that I turned to alcohol. I wasn't doing too well in school. They have the A-D-A now, but it's about 30 years too late for me. During college, my mother was diagnosed with a terminal illness. Some people talk about a higher power. You know what, my higher power was my mother. For 25 years everything revolved around her. My mother passed away in 1990. Because I grew up in an alcoholic dysfunctional family, alcohol was a natural way to cope.

When I was a young adult, living in Indianapolis, I had a hard time getting a job. A lot of the problem was because of my hearing. See, they didn't have the technology that they have now. I spent my time partying. It was good to be around people. It took me 15 years after my dad passed away to realize alcohol would not help with my depression. Surprise, surprise. You can't medicate depression with a depressant.

My job today is staying sober one day at a time. I've got about 20 years of not living the way I used to. You know, most people, when they come into the Café, they feel like it's the end of the world. But, when you get started, when you finally get it, you realize it's just the end of the old life, and the beginning of the new life.

HEALING FOR MYSELF

MALISSA'S STORY AS TOLD TO JENNA JAMESON

What initially started me coming off the needle and methamphetamines was falling in love. I didn't want him to deal with me like that, and I knew it wasn't fair for him. At the time, he was all the support I had. He removed himself from my life in 2020. The last time I got clean was for my kids, and that didn't stick. When I'd try getting clean, I'd end up relapsing, and relapsing, and relapsing. I struggled with nineteen years of drug use, with almost two years of clean time during rehab in 2008. Now, I've been in recovery for 16 months. It has to be for me this time, so I don't go back. Until you do it for yourself, you're not going to care if you go back or not.

Recovery is hard. It's a challenge. You're battling your own patterns. When I got into drug use, it slowly progressed. I started using harder drugs, in harder ways over time. It takes just as long to get out of addiction—to retrain your brain towards a positive direction—as it takes to get into it. On top of that, parts of your brain get damaged by the drugs, like your dopamine receptors and feel-good senses. It makes you impulsive, so it's not easy to choose to do the right thing. The hurt that you feel when you're going through the healing process, processing and owning the things you've done, makes you want to run. I punished myself with drugs, and masked how I felt. I ran instead of dealing with it. Because that's what you're used to doing, using drugs to numb that hurt and not feeling anything.

Drugs aren't the only thing I'm recovering from. I'm recovering from unhealed trauma, injustice from my family and foster parents, "the system," boyfriends, and myself. Really, the only person I can blame for it is myself because I allowed all of it to happen repeatedly, over and over again. I'm the only one with the power to stop it, but when you don't know what boundaries are, what they're for, how to set them, and then how to reinforce them, change can feel impossible. When I first learned about boundaries, I was angry. I suddenly realized that I was the one that had power, the whole time. The underlying emotion to anger is hurt, and I was very hurt.

The things I've gone through have left me with a lot of anxiety. The last person I told everything to used every bit of it against me. My family projected their limitations onto me. I get anxious when talking about things that I know I need to heal, because I don't trust people. The anxiety comes from one person and one person alone, me.

When I relapsed previously, it was because I tried working on all of my issues at once. I developed a sex addiction, I smoked cigarettes, and happen to have a dirty mouth and a dirty mind. I'm mouthy and speak my mind with no filter. When I tried to do everything cold turkey, it blew up, and all my bad habits made their way back in. Then, when I would finally get my footing back after a relapse, I'd go right back to trying to work on everything. Thinking and believing that I can do everything by myself, all at once, like I'm Supergirl was not a good thing for me. It doesn't work that way.

I had to change where I lived, change my surroundings, and change the people I hung out with. On January 1st of 2021, I moved to Indianapolis and started a new year and a new me within a big city. I was living at the Salvation Army Women and Children's Shelter on North Alabama Street. I asked if anybody knew where any recovery outlets were and learned about the Recovery Café in Indy. I checked it out, and I liked being somewhere where the people were either going through exactly what I was going through, or had already been through it and were trying to refrain from falling back into old patterns and habits. It was somewhere for me to meet with a group of peers to share, help lean on each other, and ultimately build each other up. It gave me help with some support in my recovery journey. On November 11th of 2022, I moved here to Muncie to the YWCA. I looked for another recovery outlet and found the Recovery Café in Muncie where I started out as a member, went to companion, then member leader, and now I'm a senior member leader and a circle facilitator. The Recovery Café has been the biggest help for my recovery outside of myself.

Ultimately, I'm doing this for me, because I want a better me. I want the whole me. I want the healed me. I want to do this for me because I have to live with that person. It doesn't matter if anyone else is around me or not. If I'm being good to myself, then I can be good to others. It's been a challenging experience, but everything is what you make of it. I just don't know how to give up.

How I Learned That I Was in Recovery

Jacob's Story as Told to Nicole Jones

I 've come to realize that I'm in recovery, and, in a sense, we all are. It was my time working with the Recovery Café that helped me to understand that. I was a sophomore at Ball State when I did the immersive learning course that partnered with Recovery Café. At first, being at the Café was a little difficult for me. It was an unfamiliar space with a lot of people. It set off some of my anxieties. Eventually, though, I was able to be comfortable there. I think it was seeing how open everyone is that made me realize what a special place it is. It really seems like everyone there has known each other for years, when it could've only been a few months or so. It seems like they're actually just one big family.

In our work with Recovery Café, my classmates and I had to propose projects that would benefit the Café's mission. My group suggested making a video to help de-stigmatize recovery and help people understand that recovery is about more than homelessness or addiction. There were several of us in the class who were media majors, so we wanted to use those skills. We created a video sharing impactful stories and highlighting how the Café supports everyone's unique recovery journey. I really threw myself into the project, I think because filmmaking is something I've always used to make sense of things. That project pushed me in a lot of ways. I spent more hours than I can count editing and revising it; I kind of spiraled at one point. Editing the interviews was intense. Hearing the people we interviewed describe their recovery made me understand what I was actually dealing with. It helped me to kind of stop and say, "yeah, I'm in recovery."

I've been diagnosed with depression since age eight, and later around thirteen or fourteen, I was diagnosed with anxiety. The depression was kind of there my whole life, haunting me. But middle school came along and that was particularly rough. I feel like anyone who has attended a middle school can say middle schoolers absolutely suck. Around that time, I discovered my passion for filmmaking, so I made pretty crappy home videos with a camcorder I got for Christmas. I uploaded some of them to YouTube under an alias. My classmates found out and picked on me. I was bullied for probably three to four years, all of middle school, and a little bit of the start of high school. Thankfully it never got physical, like slamming me into lockers or anything, but it was still pretty awful. Half of the time, they were overtly cruel. Half of the time, it took the form of condescending "niceness," where they would come up to me and act like we were buddy-buddy. That stuff would bother me to no end. I would lash out and yell and get in trouble because teachers saw what they were doing from afar and just assumed those kids were genuinely trying to be my friend. They never understood. There wasn't really anything that happened that made them stop, apart from them just getting bored. It sucks that I never really got the resolution that I needed. There is always a part of me that never got the last laugh.

It's an ongoing process still. I found a good therapist who I feel like I work well with, and I've learned some good skills to cope better and prevent myself from getting in my own head. I'm better at advocating for myself and even for what other people may need. I do my best to help others who are struggling. Those have been the big steps toward recovery for me. My goals right now are just to keep putting one foot forward, to try to stay well, and just make little bits of progress. I'm not in the headspace where I can think ahead ten years. I can just give myself a list of things I want to do today, give myself some time to breathe and some time to decompress, and then just leave it at that. I take it day by day. If I make a step forward, that's good, and if I take a step back, that's okay too.

That's where the Café helped me most. Of everyone we interviewed, not a single one of them was like, "I'm done recovering.

Book's closed, story's over." They may be out of the woods, but they don't stop there. Because recovery never stops. I realized that things aren't going to be perfect, and maybe my entire life I won't actually feel like I'm out of the depression. I have been able to make peace with that. It's important to accept the journey and the self-confrontation that recovery demands. Am I the most unfortunate guy on the face of the earth? No. Am I dealing with something absolutely horrible? No. But, it's still something I'm recovering through. Maybe it's cynical, but I think there's no silver lining in some things. Sometimes, the only thing you can do is just deal with it. But, for me, practicing gratitude has been important. Things aren't perfect, but they're much better than they used to be. I can't say, "I'm content. I'm happy." Not yet. But I'm getting there.

HEALING WHAT MY BODY HELD WITHIN

GWEN'S STORY AS TOLD TO KAMRYN GIBSON

I could see my heart beating through my chest. I couldn't eat anything. I couldn't do anything. I would lie in bed, crying, feeling at the mercy of my own body. I had no idea what was happening to me. I was 18 years old, but I weighed only 98 pounds. I couldn't even stand at my grandfather's funeral. I underwent countless tests to figure out what was wrong with me. I got a colonoscopy and endoscopy, sent in stool samples, and had blood tests. In the end, I was given a general diagnosis of a systematic inflammatory issue caused by PTSD. I thought it was a bullshit diagnosis, and I was really upset that I did not have the answers that I needed to recover.

My problems trace back to middle school. I had joined this message board for *My Little Pony*, where I encountered some over-age men. This spiraled into a three-year relationship with two of them. Looking back, I realized that many adults failed me, not only the ones who were actively preying on me, but also those who passively let it happen. I wasn't okay with what had happened, but I went through this mental turmoil of trying to accept it. I cut my hair and dyed it purple. I started wearing super goth makeup and dressing dark. At the time, the style was really helping me cope with the realities that I faced every day.

Then, in high school, I experienced assault. I was scared and unsure of how to speak up about it. My parents noticed a drastic change in my behavior. I went from being a straight A student to barely getting by with C's.

Sometime later, I was in communication with the person who assaulted me and was on the phone with them one day while I was in the shower. Suddenly, I felt lightheaded and nauseated, and everything went black. I was rushed to the hospital and diagnosed with vasovagal syncope which can present itself like a seizure but has different triggers. The doctors basically told me, "We don't know, eat better."

I went looking for a better answer. I came across an online video about Avoidant Restrictive Food Intake Disorder (ARFID) and immediately recognized the similarities with what I was experiencing. I shared this with my therapist, who agreed with the diagnosis. At that point, I finally had a name for what I was going through: ARFID. The challenge now was finding treatment. At the time, there were only two places in the United States that accepted me. Thankfully, I found a place 30 minutes away in Anderson, Indiana called Selah. In April 2022, I went to Selah and that's when I started my recovery.

When I first arrived at Selah, I was super ill, and my body was reacting badly to the treatment. I had to start off immediately eating full meals, which was a lot for me because ARFID involves a phobia to food. I was afraid of getting sick and facing health consequences like diabetes. As a child, I had convinced myself that I would die by the age of 18 because of how much sugar I ate. I also had concerns about food safety, including rotting and mold. I would throw up for hours, unintentionally, leaving me exhausted. I found it hard to believe that it was ARFID causing all these issues and I thought it could still be some sort of underlying illness. Once, the vomiting got so bad that they had to take me to the hospital again. That would be the last time that I was hospitalized.

Two weeks into residential treatment, I was doing an art therapy session that took me back to the time that I was assaulted. My therapist had me draw a to-scale outline of my body and then, using different colored crayons, mark places on the body where I felt physical pain that day. We pinned the drawing up to the wall and analyzed it. My mind went blank. I was having a really hard time. Usually, I could talk about the assault, so I was confused that this was bothering me so much. My reaction to that drawing made me realize that I had never really processed that moment—had never actually faced a lot of the emotions.

I started feeling lightheaded and throwing up. A nurse came in and handed me an icepack, instructing me to place it on my vagus nerve. It helped me to calm down. I asked her more about the vagus nerve and she explained that when you have a vasovagal syncope, your vagus nerve becomes overrun. I was like, "Oh my God. That seizure I experienced while in the shower back in high school was because of my vagus nerve."

I learned that this nerve controls anxiety, nausea, and a variety of other things. I started realizing that my body is where I hold my anxiety and trauma, and that's what was causing me to get physically sick. That was a huge moment for me. I cried with relief and happiness. I finally had the answers I had been looking for. ARFID was the *why*, and the vagus nerve was the *how*.

The things I learned about my body and my trauma make it possible for me to handle things. Now, whenever I feel anxious or nauseous, I apply a cold ice pack to my chest, or just apply pressure to calm down. This discovery has allowed me to do things I never thought was possible, and to learn how to be there for important moments in my life.

I want to share my story because I think it's relatable to other people my age. A lot of people in my age range had negative experiences with the Internet like I did, and I also believe that many people experience symptoms of ARFID and just don't know what to call it. The healthcare system can be a bureaucratic maze and it can be hard to get answers. A lot of people end up finding their diagnosis in unconventional ways like I did. I hope that this story helps someone to keep hoping even when they feel hopeless. I want people to know that things can change when you feel stuck.

THE REAL WORK OF RECOVERY

GARY'S STORY AS TOLD TO LACY COAKLEY

S taying sober is great. But being sober is not really recovery. It's a part of it, but sobriety is the smallest part. Until you face up to things, you're still the same person. The thing I had to face up to was my anger and my violent behaviors.

My biological father was really violent. He abused my mother badly. Even though he wasn't around for long, what I saw affected me. I didn't realize how much it affected me until later in life. As a preteen, I discovered my own violence, and I learned that using violence, or the threat thereof, got the results I wanted. I learned that I could manipulate my surroundings through intimidation. On top of that, I had a lot of anger because my father removed himself from my life so easily. It was a betrayal. He wanted nothing to do with me. I chased him for years. And while I had reasons to be angry, I just did not handle it well.

A lot of people paid the price for me not being able to handle it. I was married young, at 19, and the violence carried over. When you have an explosive temper, it becomes a switch, and when the switch gets flipped, it's floodgates. It's not a leak; it's the whole river. I didn't use physical violence with my family, but I did much more damage with my words, with intimidation and control, than I could have done even with physical violence. That emotional violence leaves deeper scars, bigger wounds.

23

That's why sobriety is just part of the equation for me, because the anger was there long before the addiction. I was 20 when I had the accident that injured my back and led to two major back surgeries. The opiates I was prescribed for that started me on a journey of 25 years of addiction. My pain pill addiction gave way to other drugs, even heroin. I did lots of things I regret.

Getting arrested saved my life. I spent 90 days in jail and 20 months in work release. During that time, I was clean for part of it, but then I sought out drugs at other times. At my disciplinary hearing, it was clear that I had a choice to make, or I would go to prison. I swore I was ready to make a change and, for some reason, the man deciding my fate believed me.

That was 2017, when I put the needle down, and I have stayed away from heavy drugs since then. I was totally clean for three years until 2020. Guilt and shame dragged me back in for a couple years and I battled with some other minor drugs until 2021. But that time in jail and work release was where the work began. I did AA faithfully, in part because my wife could come to AA meetings with me. I used that time to really dig into the underlying causes of my addiction and violence. I had to put a spotlight on me to make that recovery happen. I noticed that there were things that I couldn't talk about, and realized that those were the things I needed to process. It's not comfortable to sit down and face the monster inside yourself.

It's a process. For the past three years I've been focused on trying to be a better person and understand myself better. A big problem was that I didn't know myself, and I had used drugs young, so I was emotionally stunted. I'm trying to understand the effects of my actions on the people I love. My son had to step in and be a dad when he was young. My oldest daughter didn't talk to me for three years. Forgiveness is a process when you've hurt the people you love as much as I had. It's a lot of shame. I can never go back and be a good dad for them in their younger years. But I am trying to be the best dad and grandpa I can be now.

I am grateful every day that I get a chance to be different. All of my kids talk to me now and it's good to see that coming back to me. I know it seems cliché, but it's cliché for a reason. You have to be the better person for them, not for you. It's hard to go the right direction unless you do it for the people you love.

Coming to the Recovery Café, I realize that the more I give, the more I get. The payoff is better than any drug. It makes me a lot happier and fulfilled to help other people. I do peer support as a Recovery Coach. I'm a senior leader. My next goal is to do classes to become NAMI certified.

If you're honestly working through it, you need to work through it with someone else because it does get heavy. I could have the best and most caring doctor in the world, but they can't relate to this experience personally. That's why community is important, and that's why I try every day to be the best husband, father, and friend I can be. Life is happier being a servant, rather than trying to dictate things.

MAKING A DIFFERENT CHOICE

DWAYNE'S STORY AS TOLD TO COREY COOPER AND PALANI ZUSSMAN

D rug and alcohol use is a choice that you make. You can say "no" at any time. I've done it.

I've experienced homelessness. I experienced jail and prison. I've learned from those things. At some point you gotta tell yourself, "I can't do this anymore." On October the 2nd of 2021, I just said "no more." That's how I know that it is a choice that you make.

I grew up on the west side of Chicago in a family of five. My mom was a single parent. She ran a tight household. We weren't allowed to drink or anything like that as long as we were in her household. Even though she tried to keep us on the right path, I took my first drink at the age of 18. Alcohol was part of my life all the way up until two and a half years ago.

I came to Muncie in 1990 and got into my active addiction. I was just a party animal then, when I met my wife. We spent 33 years together, both battling addiction. I had to get past that, past being in a relationship with a fellow alcoholic. I had to ask myself how long I wanted to keep on doing the same thing without seeing different results.

I knew that if I wanted to get better, I had to make a different choice. In a situation like that, you are either going to stop doing what you used to do, or you are going to make up your mind and just quit. I did it. Cold Turkey. I just told myself that it's over.

The most important thing that I had to deal with was the first three steps of the 12-step program. First, I had to admit that I was an addict, that my life had become unmanageable. Second, I had to come to believe that there is a power greater than myself that can restore me back to sanity. And, three, I had to make a decision to turn my will and my life over to the care of my higher power, as I understand Him.

Recovery is not something you can do alone. I had to understand that what stood in my way was me. I'm my worst enemy, so I had to have support. Otherwise, I would just mess things up all over again. I had to let my higher power take over to get me through my recovery process, and I needed to be around the right people. I had to change the people I used to hang out with, the places I used to go, and the things I used to do. I moved from the area where I was active in my addiction, and it allowed me to think more clearly and live without constant stress.

My friend, Robert, and I dedicated ourselves to hold one another accountable. We walked this thing together, him and I. From the first day when I took that last drink, him and I walked this together.

Robert kept telling me about the Recovery Café. I was on GPS house arrest and I was skeptical about the Café, but I just decided, okay, I'm going to ask my intake officer if I can go and check it out. Once I got there, I saw the love that was down there and how family oriented it was. Everyone was supporting one another, and everyone was just communicating. I told myself, man, this will be a safe haven for me. And it has been ever since the first day I came, I have never left. Now I'm dedicated and committed.

Recovery has improved my life tremendously. Tremendously. I've been able to achieve my goal of getting my chef's license. I attended culinary arts school here at Augusta de Escoffier and I graduated May 21st of this year. I now have my license. I did it all.

I have a peace of mind now. I have inner peace. I wish my mom was living right now so she can see the dramatic change that I've made because this is for her. The transformation that I've made, she would have loved it. This is something that she always wanted. I did it not only for me. This is dedicated to her as well.

This is what happens when you get off alcohol, chase and complete your goals. I tell my story because I want people to know It can be done, if you want to do it. It's like the program says, you gotta want it. If you want it and you are dedicated in your heart, it can happen.

LIFE AFTER DEATH

DESTINI'S STORY AS TOLD TO JUAN RUIZ

J ust don't give up. That's my message to those who are reading this.

I used to play softball, baseball, and more. I loved softball so much that I played for my school team. I was in the JROTC program and my plan after high school was to be an active-duty marine. All of that was changed when I got pain pills for a dental procedure. That was my first contact with drugs and the start of my addiction.

From pain pills, I moved on to weed, heroin, and meth. In order to sustain my addiction, I would steal clothes and meat from the store. One day I was at a friend's house (or so-called friend) doing heroin. I really don't remember many details about that day. Nothing seemed out of the ordinary until I overdosed. I fell down on his sofa, and he just left me there. He did call my mom. I'll give him that. He called her and said, "Hey, your daughter is on my couch." My mom called the police, and they got the ambulance.

I died on arrival.

They revived me, but not completely. I was in a coma for a long, long time. During that time, I was on life support. They had to put a tube that went through my throat for me to breathe. During my coma, my mom would come in to visit me. She would paint and cut my nails everyday. Sometimes my dad would come with her, or my cousins. The room was always filled with people to the point that the nurses would get angry because it was too loud. But I was not able to hear or feel anything.

They gave my mom the option to unplug me, but she never gave up on me. She had faith that I would wake up. While I was in a coma, they had to do surgery on me because my brain was swelling inside my skull. They cut my skull and left a hole open. It's still there. If I ever hit that part of my head, I will die.

On the day that I woke up my hands were paralyzed, and my first thought was to get up. But as soon as I tried, an alarm went off and the nurse came rushing to my room and stopped me from getting up. Later I discovered that I had a mat underneath my bed that made an alarm go off. I tried to get up so many times that my nurse was mad at me.

I didn't stay too long in that hospital. Later, I got transferred to IU Indianapolis, where they helped me quit drugs. Rehab was hard. But now I've been clean for 10 years, since I woke up from my coma until now.

I use a wheelchair now. At the beginning, it was hard to get used to. I've been going to physical therapy where they help me walk. I live in a nursing home. I always wanted an apartment and I can't have that, but I'm lucky to be alive. My memory has been affected, too. I see myself as Lucy from the movie *50 First Dates*.

Now I've been going to the Recovery Café in downtown Muncie. Laura, from the nursing home told me to check it out. I like the Café. I feel at home and the people are nice. From the moment I arrived, I felt at home. The people are kind, and the community is uplifting.

Now, I take life one day at a time. Every day when I wake up, I remind myself how far I've come and how lucky I am to still be here. Recovery is a journey, and though it's not always easy, it's worth it. I've found hope, strength, and a sense of belonging at the Recovery Café, and for that, I'm grateful.

A WARRIOR HEART AND A FRIENDLY SMILE

CAT'S STORY AS TOLD TO JOEY PHILPOTT

M y full name is Melodie Catherine Meier, but everyone calls me Cat. I think what people notice about me is that I'm usually pretty happy and excited, with a smile on my face no matter if it's early morning or late at night. But there's a lot more to my story than most people would guess.

Back in 2019, just before the pandemic hit, I moved from Toledo to Indianapolis and things started going really wrong for me. I met someone at a shelter who became my roommate. The first year living together was fine. I mean, we argued sometimes, like roommates do, but I didn't think much of it. But then toward the end of that year, everything changed. She began physically beating me, mentally and emotionally abusing me, calling me names—everything you can think of. One time she beat me so badly that the whole left side of my face was swollen up. I couldn't even go to work. She threatened that if I told anyone—my parents, people at work, anyone at church—she'd find me wherever I was and put me six feet under the ground.

I was too afraid to tell anyone for a long time, but, finally, I couldn't take it anymore. I told my mom and dad what was happening. They freaked out and took me straight to the police station to file a report. But the police weren't much help. They said since she was just my

31

roommate and not family or a romantic partner, they didn't even consider it domestic violence. I was like, "Seriously? How is this not domestic violence?" All they told me was to file a protection order, and they said I could press charges if I wanted to. I filed that protection order against her and her cousin, who would watch as she beat me. I found out later my roommate had been in jail three or four times for the same thing. When I moved out, my parents tried to take me to a shelter, but it was the same place where I'd met my roommate. She was threatening me, so I knew I couldn't stay there. That's when I decided to disappear.

I ended up living under a bridge for three months. It was complete terror. There was a homeless community, and cops would drive by all the time. Every night I had to find a quiet, safe place to pitch my tent, then pack everything up in the morning so nobody would steal my stuff. Just trying to find somewhere clean to wash up and something to eat every day was a struggle. One day, my stepdad's cousin found me living under that bridge and brought me to their house for the night. I knew I needed to do something.

Finally, on August 22nd, 2021, I called 211. That's the resource number for anyone dealing with homelessness. I told them I was in a domestic situation and needed to get out of Indianapolis because I was scared for my life. They directed me to the YWCA (the Y) in Muncie, where there was an opening. I packed up two weeks' worth of stuff, which was all they allowed, and my cousin drove me to Muncie. For the first week, I stayed in their emergency overnight program. Then, I met with my case manager and got moved into their 45-day program. For the first time in a while, I had my own room with a bed and TV.

At the Y, I met a young lady who was coming to the Recovery Café, which is just down the street. I started going all the time. I became a full member and then I went through all the different programs here: the companion program, the member program, and the member leader program. I eventually became a senior member leader.

Recovery Café is not what you might expect. A lot of people, when they first hear "recovery," they think it's just for addiction. But that's one of the big misconceptions about this place. We accept people in any form of recovery, from addiction to mental health stuff to domestic violence. Even just being lonely. It's a special place. The second you walk in upstairs and get off the elevator, you just feel such a warm and welcoming glow.

I'm in recovery from mental health stuff myself—major depressive disorder, social anxiety, bipolar II, ADHD, and general anxiety. I've actually struggled with my mental health since I was about 12, but it wasn't until I came here that I really got diagnosed and started getting the help I needed. I didn't even realize how much help I needed. When I first moved to Muncie, I wouldn't go out on my own. I'd only go out with groups of ladies I had made friends with at the Y. And even then, I'd be looking over my shoulder constantly. In my new place, sometimes I think I hear her hollering my name, especially when I'm alone. When I tell people that, they say I'm crazy, but I am not. I'm just still trying to recover from a domestic situation. Now I can recognize my triggers and handle things better. December 12th will mark three years since I started actually getting help. That's what I consider my recovery date.

Sometimes I still struggle, but things have gotten better in ways I never expected. Less than a year after coming here, I went back to school at Ivy Tech. See, meeting all the young ladies at the Y and hearing their stories about what brought them there, and their different recovery stories, made me realize there aren't very many resources to help young women dealing with domestic violence, homelessness, or substance abuse problems. There aren't many resources for teens in the same situation either. I wanted to be part of helping them, just like others helped me.

On January 17th, thanks to the Y, A Better Way, and Meridian, I got my own place. They set me up with a case manager and a skills builder through Meridian Health Services, and helped me get on the list for public housing. They helped with the cost of housing and utilities for a year. I still struggle here and there to pay bills, like everybody does. But I'm happy. I wear my Ivy Tech lanyard and hoodie proudly, excited about helping others to change their lives just like I changed mine. Sometimes I think about how if I hadn't gone through that terrible situation, I probably wouldn't be the person I am today. I've learned that if you need help, you shouldn't be afraid to ask questions or ask for help. That's what recovery is really about— knowing you're not alone.

PANTRIES, HEARTS, AND HOW TO FILL THEM

CALLIE'S STORY AS TOLD TO LILIBETH TERRAZAS

W hen I first visited the Recovery Café, I wanted to run back up the stairs. I'm not gonna lie about that one. You walk in and it's a really homey environment, but coming from a small town in Indiana and being a college student, I was out of my element. In those first uncomfortable moments at the Café, I never imagined what a big impact the experience would eventually have on me.

Since the visits to Recovery Café were pre-planned, there was no choice but to engage with the members and try to get past the awkwardness. It was important to try to connect. We were there to listen and try to understand what people needed, so we could propose a project that would support the Café's mission. I'd say that it was our third visit when everyone started to get comfortable. At that specific visit, we did Bingo and it was, oh my gosh, it was so loud in there. Everyone in the center was chit-chatting with each other because, by then, we had all gotten comfortable and started to open up about personal stuff.

On one of our visits, the Café manager had given us a tour of the facility and shared background information on the Café's mission and what type of activities the members of the Café were able to engage in. The manager showed us a pantry for food and clothes they had just started to provide relief for members who experience homelessness or food insecurity. The pantry was pretty much empty at the time, so my group saw that as a need we could help with. Our conversations with the members confirmed that many of them didn't have access to enough quality food to meet their basic needs.

My classmate, Morgan, and I spent so many hours outside of class on this project. It was our baby. We made phone calls all over campus and in town, asking for permission to leave donation boxes. We were constantly checking in with each other. We both have always engaged in volunteer work, which is why I believe we gravitated towards this project so much. My parents raised me with the mindset of if you have time, go volunteer, because someone else will need and appreciate the help. No one ever really knows what anyone is going through and if you have the time to help others, then do it because it could impact someone.

This experience was special because we actually got to know the people we were serving. After receiving enough donations, we collected the items and brought them to the Café. The members were so nice. They made us feel like it was Christmas and they just got a bunch of presents put in front of them. My group and I went into this thinking we were going to be able to fill their pantry about six different times, but it wasn't like that. I wished we could have done more. But I feel like we got the things they really wanted. We sat down and listened. We got a list of all the foods they wanted and that's what we asked donors for. Soups or ramen noodles were their first request. And then from there we got what we could, and we filled it up. When they saw everything full, they were excited, even relieved. I don't want to say it was emotional, but the experience made the problem of food insecurity real for me.

At the end of the course, we had a meeting at the Café where we shared information on our projects. This meeting was the most memorable part for me because we had started out getting to know people and we talked to the members one on one. We had about seven or eight visits, but our last visit was a wrap-up where everyone was there. Our whole class, our professor, the food pantry intern, and about fifteen to twenty members were present for this meeting. We discussed everything we did during the course, and we came up with a plan on how to continue our projects. It was a great way to end our project. It didn't feel like, just because the project was over, our connection to the Café was done. The members encouraged us to come back. They said, "We want to see you again, you guys are always welcome here."

Since then, I continue to visit them and drop off necessities. Anytime I see someone post that they are getting rid of clothes, I let them know that I'll take it and then I drive it over to the Café.

I can't fully explain how this experience changed my perspective. Being in this class and meeting the members of the Café helped me to understand other people's hardships. The work we did was more than a project for me and my classmates. It was a big eye-opener for a lot of us, and it is definitely something that I still talk about all the time.

FINDING REASONS TO HOLD ON

BRETT'S STORY AS TOLD TO TONY ORTA

I don't remember a time in my life when I wasn't around drugs. I was about two or three years old when I walked in on my third oldest brother helping my dad shoot up. I can't recall exactly where it was, but I do remember my mom flipping out when she found them. She called the cops and I remember her yelling. Just before the cops came, my father snuck away and hid the rig and everything inside the big 1960's phone we had. When the cops showed, they couldn't find anything. That was my introduction to heroin.

Years later, after my father left, I started to hold it down for my brother, watching him go through the high and the fall. I watched him to make sure nothing went wrong. I didn't start using then, but I did later on. Using led to the worst things that have happened to me and I spend every day trying to get past it.

I was eight when I first started smoking weed, and I can't recall when I started drinking. I had three older brothers and I looked up to them. We used to fight one another, steal, and skip school together. It was a hard time in my life living in Boston, but an even harder time for my mom. She had to manage us, and deal with her own problems too. In our home, they were all functional alcoholics, except my mom. She used to have a hard time holding down a job, but she never gave up. For a while she had a job at the jail, making sure the inmates got back to their cells. I was going in and out of jail at the time, and she got the job from one of my parole officers. He knew our family pretty well, if that says anything to you. When my mom found out that she had Multiple Sclerosis, her hands became too shaky with the keys, so they let her go.

When I was a senior in high school, I got in trouble again and was sent to jail, but this was the time of graduation. I met all the requirements for graduation, so I was in the county jail for ten days. I was released so I could walk, but then they put me back in for six months to serve the rest of my time. Even though that was a shit show, I was the only one out of all my older brothers to finish high school. I think that was part of what set me on the wrong path—getting caught up in the wrong system from the start.

By 1989, I was finally sick of it all, going in and out of jail, being around the wrong crowd, and, overall, just feeling stuck. My mom sent me to live with my brother in Muncie. Some time passed and I was doing good for a while in my new life in Muncie. It started to go downhill again when I was with my second wife. She was a spark of life that I was glad I got to get to know, but then again, I started to shoot up heroin and smoke crack when I was with her. She never made me do anything but after some time being around it and not knowing how to control myself, I started to use with her. In three years, all of my teeth had fallen out and I had overdosed a total of five times.

A lot happened before we split in 2023, but the thing that changed everything was the death of her brother. He used to come over to get high because he knew I had stuff. I still had an issue with stealing and I managed to get a lot this one time: coke, weed, heroin, you name it. But this one time, I was hanging with a friend and my brother-in-law. I usually only gave my brother-in-law weed so there was no harm, but he said he wanted to try something different. I could tell he had been on speed, so he had that high going on when he wanted to try something new. My friend said that I should give him some. I was very hesitant at first because I knew what could happen. I don't know if it was the peer pressure or if it was the environment I was in, but I gave in.

I took out a bag of fentanyl and tried to pull out the smallest amount I could. Not even a second later he sniffed it and we waited. After watching his high and fall, I thought that was the end of it. But he started to get sick after a couple of hours. He threw up and, after some time, both my friend and I knew he was not gonna be okay. We called the cops and we carried him outside so they could reach him faster.

Before I knew it, he was gone. He lay in my arms and I thought, "What have I done?" As the police showed up, he was still lying in my arms. They questioned me and I told them everything. I asked to be taken away. I felt like I killed him. It was my fault. But the cops insisted nothing was going to happen. Six months later, I received in the mail a warrant for my arrest: four D-level felonies, one misdemeanor, and two counts of child neglect.

I am still under probation today for what happened then, and it was a major reason why I started coming to the Recovery Café. It helps finding people that understand the pain of being an addict. Most of the time, this is a space where I can share my story, feel heard, and also find some help when I need it most. It's not always like that. Sometimes this place can make me feel like using again—being around certain people that I know are still getting high.

But I am finding my reasons to hold on. And even if I can't do it for myself, I will do it for someone else. My daughter has helped me so much, more than she will ever know, although, it is hard seeing her grow and leave me behind. All the events in her life gave me reasons to stay alive. I just wanted to be here so that I can see them happen. Substance abuse is something that never goes away fully, I think. It's always an ongoing battle. Some days, I feel like it would be better if I didn't wake up, and other days, I get excited to watch a new movie or something like that.

I started at a young age. I've been surrounded by people using all my life. I almost died five or six times. Even through it all, I am still finding my reasons to live. I just hope my story can show it's possible to keep going.

Finding Help After Burnout

An Anonymous Story as Told to Meah Griswold

Y ou can't expect yourself to do the unreasonable. I've learned that the hard way this semester. I've always known I tend to pile things onto my plate until I am overwhelmed, but this semester, I pushed myself to the point of burnout. Thankfully, the people at the Recovery Café were there for me when it all hit.

I was introduced to the Café through an immersive learning course I took at Ball State University in 2023. I accidentally took the immersive section, not realizing what it was at the time, and I was definitely nervous to start. I had been extremely withdrawn from the world for several years at that time and had not been that involved within the community even longer. Honestly, I wasn't sure if I could do it, but I stuck with it.

I don't remember exactly when I truly fell in love with the Café, but I do remember one visit in particular. I was sitting at a table with a couple different members, and they were all just being honest about what they had gone through, and how that has affected them today. I had never experienced such honesty when there had been so much struggle. One person at that table was actively experiencing withdrawal. What caught my eye, was that not one person saw him negatively. The people around him were supporting him, and helping him the best way that they could. There was no shame. I remember he was beating himself up because he hadn't been able to stay clean long enough to be able to see his daughter. At that moment, it was like everything flipped for me. I realized that there had been so much negativity and stigma relating to addiction ingrained in me for so long.

After that, I did everything I could to be in the Café. My class worked on a project to help refill the pantry, through a food drive and a fundraiser. All of my work was unfortunately done outside of the Café, but I remember that whole semester I was just wishing I could get back into the Café, back working directly with people. I was scared to do it by myself though. I had always gone with peers in my class before. However, summer semester courses required 10 hours of Service Learning, which meant 10 hours of volunteering. I thought, I'll just go to the Café and do those hours. I did those 10 hours within about two months, and it was amazing. I kept going. And before I knew it, I was well beyond my 10 hours.

I have met people at the Café who are struggling with substance use disorder, with trauma, homelessness, domestic violence, and sometimes a combination of all of them. There were also those who struggled with their mental health. I've dealt with depression and severe anxiety my whole life, and to be around people who normalized and humanized it made me feel very seen.

I had a rocky start to this semester. I was working two part-time jobs, a Resident Hall Association Representative and Hall Council member for my dorm, a full-time student that had gotten accepted into nursing school, and I was volunteering at the Café three days a week. In my personal life, I was dealing with the sudden loss of my grandfather, and then, in the middle of everything, my partner of four years and I broke up. On one hand, I was so involved in so many cool experiences. On the other hand, life just kept kicking me. I was doing the best I could with everything that was happening, while also trying to avoid everything that was happening.

Eventually, I reached a breaking point. I had a bad reaction to one of my medications. It gave me insomnia, panic attacks, and blood pressure spikes. I was truly exhausted. I was barely eating or sleeping. I am not someone who cries a lot but I couldn't make it through a day without absolutely sobbing.

One night, when I was working a late shift at the anatomy lab, I didn't think that I was going to be able to make it through my shift. I stepped out of the lab, called my dad, and all I could say was that I just wanted to go home. He convinced me not to drop out of school, but I quit my job that night, as well as the Residence Hall Association and Hall Council.

Some of the members at the Café noticed me starting to struggle a lot more and began checking in on me. Working in the pantry I usually had the same few tasks I needed to get done every time I came in. If I was really exhausted and struggling, and wasn't able to get any work done, everyone asked how they could help. If I needed to rant, cry, or talk, someone was there to listen. If I went there and I said, "I am struggling today," they helped. They always met me where I was at. And I don't think that is something that you experience in the daily world outside of an environment like that. That was it. There was no shame.

Later on, I spoke to one of the members from the Café about how I had been doing. I had never experienced so much sheer exhaustion before and I was scared. He simply said, "I think you are experiencing burnout. Like, serious burnout." That was the first time I think I realized just how badly I needed help. He ended up giving me some serious life advice that allowed me to make it through the rest of my semester. On the days that you wake up, and you feel like crap, you don't want to do anything, you want to lie in bed and just feel bad. Those days, you get out of bed, you do whatever you absolutely need to get done, and then you can go back to bed. That's it. For the rest of the semester, I woke up every single morning telling myself, "I just have to make it through my lecture, then I can go back to bed." It seems so small, but it worked. It got me through the rest of my semester and continues to get me through the really tough days, even after.

Burnout takes time to recover from, so I am taking it bit by bit. I am beyond grateful to have had the Café during this time in my life, and cannot wait to continue seeing the growth of both myself and others at the Café.

FROM EXISTING TO LIVING

ABBY'S STORY AS TOLD TO
LILLIAN AGRUE AND KATHRYN LUDWIG

I 've experienced three different Abbys. There was young Abby, who didn't have a voice and conformed to the values and beliefs of those around her. There was Defensive Abby, who swallowed the naive and vulnerable girl in order to protect herself from the world. I would like to introduce you to Recovery Abby, who has accepted and healed from her trauma, has accepted and learned to love herself, and now gives back to those who seek peace and stability.

I grew up in Pennsylvania in a very small town with my parents and two older brothers. I was raised in the Catholic Church and went to Catholic school until 8th grade. There were four of us in that class, so that school was very, very small. When I graduated from 8th grade, I transitioned to a bigger high school, and it was a lot to take in. It was a culture shock really. I think that is when I first began to experience anxiety on a deeper level. This was the start of my mental health journey. There was a point when I was best friends with someone who dealt with the early stages of schizophrenia. At 15 years old, I took on a lot of responsibility for that person. When they had bad days or would self-harm, I took on blame for that. This led to depressive episodes and feelings of chronic guilt.

When I graduated high school, I attended a small college in

Pennsylvania to study psychology and run track. There, I was exposed to different types of people from different walks of life, which was amazing. At 21, I got out of a long-term relationship, and at that time, I was not mature enough to realize that I would be okay by myself. That break-up had a negative effect on me. Then, two months later, I was sexually assaulted at a college party. That is when life took a turn for the worse. For the next year and a half, I spent most of my time at an off-campus house with people I thought were my friends, doing drugs, drinking, missing class, and internalizing this horrible thing that had happened to me. I didn't want to think about the assault, feel the negative emotions, or talk about it, so I drank or took any substance that would numb that experience from my mind. I struggled to communicate with my family, and although they were worried about me, I wasn't ready to face the reality of the situation just yet.

In 2018, at my lowest point mentally, I was ready to give up. My psychiatrist at the time had prescribed me multiple mood stabilizers, because he was sure I had bipolar disorder. Later I found out that I am not bipolar, I was just self-medicating with uppers and downers so often, that stability was not possible. I was just existing at this time, and I didn't want to give up, but I was so tired of feeling so tired. Somehow, I found some courage to push through. I went home and asked my parents for help. It was a heavy and difficult conversation, but I knew I had to finally face the truth: I needed help. After that, I went to stay at a mental health crisis center for a week. When I got off the mood stabilizers and was prescribed the right medication, I was finally at a place where I could stop existing and begin healing.

My recovery began after discharging from the crisis center and moving back home. My healing journey has brought out things that I didn't even realize I needed to work on. The therapy continued, as well as following my medication regimen. I wasn't just existing anymore, but I was actually living a meaningful life. I was finally at a place where I moved into my own apartment, was working a great job, and started working towards my bachelor's degree again. I thought I was "fixed," but then I started abusing Adderall. I soon realized that I had a very poor relationship with food and my body. I was restricting food, constantly taking stimulants, and working out all the time. This unhealthy behavior was taking up all the space in my mind, and I finally realized that I needed change.

In 2020, I went to visit my best friend who was living in Muncie, going to Ball State. I met her circle of friends, and I felt like I had found my people, the ones I never had in college. At this time, I came to a realization; being at home was making me hold onto the trauma I had experienced. I found positivity and healing in Muncie, so much so, that I stopped taking Adderall and started focusing on my healing journey even more. I decided I needed to get out of there, so I officially moved to Muncie in 2021.

One year into living in Muncie, I started my job at Recovery Café. The Café has changed my entire perspective on life: on people, myself, addiction and mental health, and recovery in general. I've seen how a raw human experience and human connection can impact people. I love seeing people from all walks of life share their stories and encourage one another. I share from my own experience that sometimes you need to change the people, places, and things that you surround yourself with in order to recover.

Trauma is very, very interesting. It's a grey storm cloud that takes over your entire being, and I'm so thankful I had the support that I did to overcome and heal from it.

DISCUSSING THIS TOPIC IN YOUR COMMUNITY

Because The Facing Project is steeped in empathy and connecting across differences, *Listening Circles* are a fantastic way to bring more people into the conversation on the topics/themes addressed in this book.

Listening Circles provide readers with a more intimate experience to reflect upon the stories and ask questions in a controlled environment. However, it's important to include a trained facilitator who understands how to moderate, when to let conversations flow, and when to step in to move them along.

If you choose to include *Listening Circles* in your community, we recommend having at least four different locations and dates for these to happen, and be sure to have folks register in advance. Hosts could include area libraries, schools, and/or colleges and universities.

Also, it's important to set the following standards at the beginning of each discussion:

1. We acknowledge that we are all here to learn with open hearts and open minds.

2. Before speaking or asking a question, we all agree that we will take a moment to reflect on if "my voice/question matters in

the particular moment" or if "I should give the opportunity to someone else to speak."

3. R-E-S-P-E-C-T is more than an Aretha Franklin song; respect is a value that we will hold close throughout our discussions.

4. We honor the storytellers who shared their experiences, and our goal is to not discount them but rather to understand how all of our stories are intertwined and part of the human condition.

Ideally, *Listening Circles* should have no more than 20 participants in each circle. If you find that one of your locations may have more than 20, you'll want to explore breaking them up into more than one group.

Also, participants should have read a copy of this book before participating. This makes for deeper discussion, and it keeps the facilitators from having to give a full breakdown of all of the themes/topics included throughout the book. More copies can be ordered at www.facingproject.com.

However, it's always good to open a *Listening Circle* with a reading of one or two stories that immediately follow introductions and community standards. Ask for one to two attendees to volunteer to read the selected stories aloud to the *Circle*.

Then have the facilitator ask the group: How did those two stories make you feel?

And be sure to have them follow-up with "tell me more" and other open-ended questions. Of course, a trained facilitator will understand how to let this process flow. Lastly, be sure to include action items for the participants. This could include other events in your community centered around the topic/issues addressed in this book, volunteer opportunities with nonprofits, and/or other ways they can get involved.

DISCUSSION QUESTIONS

1. Was there a story that resonated with you? Which one, and why?

2. The storytellers featured in this collection understand their recoveries differently. What are some of the definitions of "recovery" articulated in these stories?

3. What surprised you the most?

4. Were any of your existing beliefs or attitudes about recovery, or people in recovery, challenged by reading these stories?

5. Has reading these stories helped you to reconsider any of your own life experiences?

6. Do you feel that you have a recovery story?

7. What examples of resilience stood out to you and why?

8. Which story leaves you wondering "what happens next?"

9. How can family be a help and a hindrance in storytellers' recovery journeys?

10. How do you see stigma as a barrier to recovery in these stories?

11. What did you learn about the impact of shame and guilt on

recovery?

12. Do you think recovery can be "completed" or is it always ongoing? Why? Which story or stories lead you to think this?

13. Why do you think the Cafe's community is able to support positive growth for members?

14. What have you learned about how to support others in their recovery?

15. What changes would you like to see in your community as a result of reading?

RESOURCES FOR RECOVERY

CHILDREN AND FAMILY
- Family Resource Center, Delaware County: Family Resource Centers (strengtheninginfamilies.org)

- Firefly: Children and Family Alliance (fireflyin.org)

DOMESTIC AND WORKPLACE SEXUAL ASSAULT
- Helping Survivors (helpingsurvivors.org/)

- A Better Way Muncie (abetterwaymuncie.org)

EDUCATION AND TRAINING OPPORTUNITIES
- Eastern Indiana Works, Workforce (easternindianaworks.org/)

- The Excel Center (excelcenter.org/)

EMPLOYMENT
- Eastern Indiana Works (easternindianaworks.org/)

- Vocational Rehab (in.gov/fssa/ddrs/)

FOOD AND CLOTHING
- Recovery Café Muncie (recoverycafemuncie.org/)
- Muncie Mission (munciemission.org/programs/food-pantry/)
- Christian Ministries (christianministriesmuncie.org)
- Soup Kitchen of Muncie (soupkitchenofmuncie.org/)

HEALTH CARE
- Open Door Health Services (opendoorhs.org/)
- Meridian Health Services (meridianhs.org)

HOUSING AND SHELTER
- Muncie Housing Authority (muncieha.com)
- Indiana Community Action Alliance (incap.org)
- Trustee's Office, Township Assistance Program in Muncie IN (rentassistance.org)
- Christian Ministries (christianministriesmuncie.org)
- Energy Assistance Program (www.in.gov/ihcda/)
- Muncie HUB (munciemission.org/programs/the-hub/)
- YWCA Central Indiana (ywcacentralindiana.org/)
- Muncie Mission (https://www.munciemission.org/)

LGBTQIA
- Muncie OUTreach (muncieoutreach.org)
- Muncie Queer Alliance (munciequeeralliance.org)
- Indiana Trans Youth Families Allies (www.imaTYFA.org)

MENTAL HEALTH AND ADDICTION

- Meridian Women's Recovery Home (meridianhs.org)

- IU Health Addictions Treatment and Recovery Center (iuhealth.org/find-medical-services/addiction-treatment)

- CleanSlate Outpatient Services (cleanslatecenters.com)

- Groups Recovering Together: Muncie Substance Use Counseling & Addiction Treatment (joingroups.com)

- Centerstone (centerstone.org/)

- NA Meetings (na.org/meetingsearch/)

- AA Meetings (aamuncie.org/)

ABOUT RECOVERY CAFÉ MUNCIE

Recovery Café Muncie is a 501(c)(3) nonprofit that supports development of the mind, body and spirit of individuals desiring recovery by creating a community committed to love, support, equality, and inclusion. Through a connected community, members of the Café sustain long-term recovery with a goal of not simply survival but becoming thriving members who reach their full potential. Our values are to connect with love in ourselves and others; show respect; cultivate compassion; practice forgiveness; encourage growth; and give back.

- Learn more at recoverycafemuncie.org

- Follow us on Instagram @recoverycafe_muncie and on Facebook at *RecoveryCafeMuncie*

ABOUT THE FACING PROJECT

The Facing Project is a 501(c)(3) nonprofit that creates a more understanding and empathetic world through stories that inspire action. The organization provides tools and a platform for everyday individuals to share their stories, connect across differences, and begin conversations using their own narratives as a guide. The Facing Project has engaged more than 7,500 volunteer storytellers, writers, and actors who have told more than 2,000 stories that have been used in grassroots movements, in schools, and in government to inform and inspire action.

In addition, stories from The Facing Project are published in books through The Facing Project Press and are regularly performed on *The Facing Project Radio Show* on NPR.

- Learn more at facingproject.com.

- Follow us on X and Instagram @FacingProject, and on Facebook at TheFacingProject.

SPONSORS

BALL STATE
UNIVERSITY
Office of Immersive Learning

www.ingramcontent.com/pod-product-compliance
Ingram Content Group UK Ltd.
Pitfield, Milton Keynes, MK11 3LW, UK
UKHW041336070325
4899UKWH00039B/1226